EXTREME JOBS IN EXTREME PLACES

LIFE ON A
SUBMARINE

By Mark Harasymiw

Gareth Stevens
Publishing

Please visit our website, www.garethstevens.com. For a free color catalog of all our high-quality books, call toll free 1-800-542-2595 or fax 1-877-542-2596.

Library of Congress Cataloging-in-Publication Data

Harasymiw, Mark.
Life on a submarine / Mark Harasymiw.
    p. cm. — (Extreme jobs in extreme places)
 Includes index.
ISBN 978-1-4339-8503-4 (pbk.)
ISBN 978-1-4339-8504-1 (6-pack)
ISBN 978-1-4339-8502-7 (library binding)
1. Submarines (Ships)—United States—Juvenile literature. I. Title.
 V858.H47 2013
 623.825'7—dc23

                              2012031424

First Edition

Published in 2013 by
Gareth Stevens Publishing
111 East 14th Street, Suite 349
New York, NY 10003

Copyright © 2013 Gareth Stevens Publishing

Designer: Andrea Davison-Bartolotta
Editor: Therese M. Shea

Photo credits: Cover, p. 1 Greg Mathieson/Time Life Pictures/Getty Images; p. 4 Boris Starosta/Stock Illustration Source/Getty Images; courtesy of the U.S. Navy: p. 5 Paul Farley, p. 7 Mass Communication Specialist 2nd Class Petty Officer April Currie, p. 9 Chief Mass Communication Specialist Dean Lohmeyer, p. 11 Photographer's Mate 2nd Class David C. Duncan, p. 12 Mass Communication Specialist Seaman Kelvin Edwards, p. 14 Photographer's Mate 3rd Class Aaron Burd, p. 16 William Kenny, p. 17 General Dynamics Electric Boat, p. 18 Mass Communication Specialist 1st Class James Kimber, p. 21 Mass Communication Specialist 2nd Class Chris Williamson, p. 22 Mass Communication Specialist 2nd Class Jeff Troutman, p. 23 Mass Communication Specialist 3rd Class Jennifer S. Kimball, p. 25 Mass Communication Specialist 3rd Class Walter M. Wayman, p. 28 US Navy, p. 29 Machinist Mate 3rd Class Sean Phillips; p. 8 Yale Joel/Time Life Pictures/Getty Images; p. 10 Anton Balazh/Shutterstock.com; p. 11 (inset) Robert D. Young/Shutterstock.com; p. 13 courtesy of U.S. Navy Petty Officer 1st Class David C. Lloyd via Wikimedia Commons; p. 15 courtesy of Agência Brasil via Wikimedia Commons; p. 19 Stocktrek Images/Thinkstock; p. 24 courtesy of PHC L.F. Stearly via Wikimedia Commons; p. 26 SuperStock/Getty Images; p. 27 Jeff Rotman/The Image Bank/Getty Images..

Printed in the United States of America

CPSIA compliance information: Batch #CW13GS: For further information contact Gareth Stevens, New York, New York at 1-800-542-2595.

CONTENTS

Words in the glossary appear in **bold** type the first time they are used in the text.

COME ABOARD

Imagine working in a three-story, windowless building that's a bit longer than a football field. Now fill it with more than 100 people, and add a **nuclear reactor** and weapons. Place that building underwater for months at a time. When you serve on a US Navy submarine, that's what your workplace and home are like!

Every sailor on a submarine has already been to at least 7 weeks of navy basic training and has asked to serve on a submarine. They've been tested to make sure they can live in tight, enclosed spaces. They've also attended special schools to learn skills they'll need on board.

For years, only men could serve on navy submarines. Women began serving on them in 2011.

AN 18-HOUR DAY

Life on a navy submarine is so extreme that the day is 18 hours long rather than 24. The crew is split into three "watch sections." Each section is on duty for 6 hours. Then they have 12 hours off. During that time, they eat, study, play games, watch movies, exercise, and sleep.

SUBMARINERS

On their first voyage, a navy submarine crewmember is called a "nub" (nonuseful body). Over a period of time, the crewmember studies and learns about all the submarine's different systems. This is so that the crew can perform well in **emergency** situations and do each other's jobs if needed. Once the crewmember passes certain tests, they become a "qual" (qualified in submarines).

Jobs on board include electricians, engineers, reactor **technicians**, weapons technicians, **sonar** operators, **navigators**, cooks, and supply specialists. The crew is led by a commanding officer and an executive officer, who's second in command.

UNDERWATER DEPARTMENTS

The navy divides submariners into different departments. The executive department focuses on management and organization. The engineering department maintains the nuclear reactor and other machinery. The weapons department handles **torpedoes** and **missiles**. The operations department focuses on navigation and communication. Finally, the supply department handles anything the crew needs, from food to machine parts.

Crewmembers on a submarine are called submariners. They're trained so well that each can operate and repair any systems and **equipment** on board.

AIR AND WATER

Submarines couldn't go far without air and water. Early submarines once had to surface to pull in fresh air. Modern submarines can stay underwater for several months. They have machines to make fresh air and water.

Machines called scrubbers remove carbon dioxide from the old air. Dust and other pollution are taken out, too. Then, electricity splits water molecules, or tiny bits of water, to free the oxygen needed to make fresh air.

Fresh water is made from seawater, which has been **distilled** to remove salt and other matter. Crewmembers called machinist mates are responsible for the air and water systems on a submarine.

THE TRITON

In 1960, the US submarine *Triton* completed the first voyage around the world entirely underwater. It began in the Atlantic Ocean, passed Cape Horn on the tip of South America, and traveled through the Pacific and Indian Oceans. It then rounded the Cape of Good Hope on the southern tip of Africa and returned to the Atlantic. The journey took 84 days.

Water, air, and power aren't a problem on a navy submarine. Sometimes it only needs to go ashore for food!

UP AND DOWN

Machinist mates and other engineers are also responsible for the systems that float or sink the submarine. Submarines have ballast tanks to help them go under or up to the surface. The ballast tanks are filled with air when a submarine is on the surface. If the submarine needs to go underwater, or submerge, water is let in to the bottom of the ballast tanks and air is let out. Since water is heavier than air, the submarine goes underwater.

Different tanks, called trim tanks, can be filled with a mix of water and air. The mix controls the depth of the submarine between the seafloor and the surface.

▲ air engine to fill ballast tanks

HYDROPLANES

A submerged submarine can be brought to the surface in several ways. One is by filling the ballast tanks with air, so the submarine becomes lighter and rises to the surface. Crewmembers called planesmen can also position the hydroplanes, which are like wings, so that the submarine is pushed to the surface by its spinning **propeller**.

propeller

NAVIGATION AND SONAR

Navigation technicians use charts, computers, and GPS (global positioning system) to aid in guiding the submarine. They also work with sonar operators.

Submarines mainly use passive sonar. This type of sonar "listens" to the sounds produced by objects in the ocean around the submarine. A sonar operator can conclude information from these sounds, such as the type and speed of a ship.

When using active sonar, a sonar operator sends a sound into the water—a "ping." The sonar operator listens to the echo to learn about the objects around the submarine. This helps the operator know how close the submarine is to the ocean floor, too.

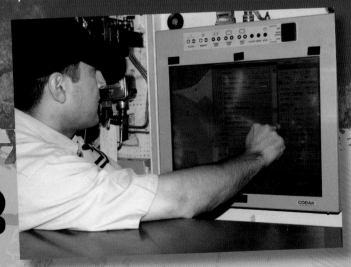

◀ computerized navigation system

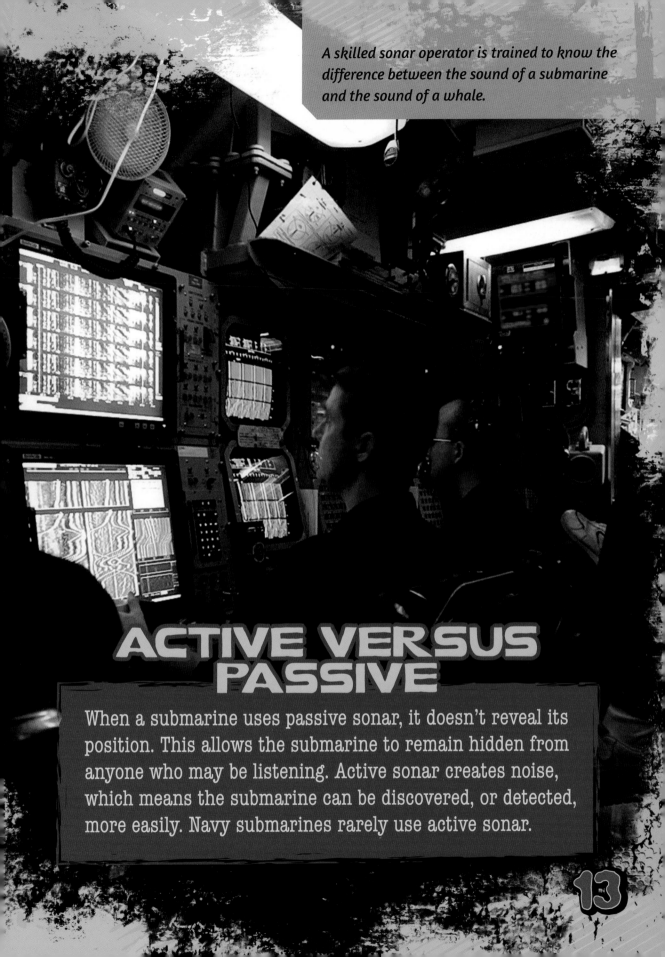

A skilled sonar operator is trained to know the difference between the sound of a submarine and the sound of a whale.

ACTIVE VERSUS PASSIVE

When a submarine uses passive sonar, it doesn't reveal its position. This allows the submarine to remain hidden from anyone who may be listening. Active sonar creates noise, which means the submarine can be discovered, or detected, more easily. Navy submarines rarely use active sonar.

NUCLEAR POWER

You've probably heard of nuclear bombs. They work through the process of **fission**. Almost all US Navy submarines today are powered by nuclear reactors. Reactors also use fission to create energy that heats water and makes steam. These things are needed to run engines and generators.

Many skilled and alert submariners are needed to maintain a submarine's nuclear reactor. There's even a Navy Nuclear Power School that trains crew for working with this equipment. Reactor technicians watch for dangerous leaks. Every submarine has a specially trained **welder** to do emergency repairs to the reactor.

RADIATION

Besides power, a nuclear reactor gives off harmful energy called radiation. You might think crew working near the reactor would be in danger. Luckily, the reactor has a shield around it to keep the crew safe. In fact, submariners are exposed to less radiation than if they were outside on a sunny day!

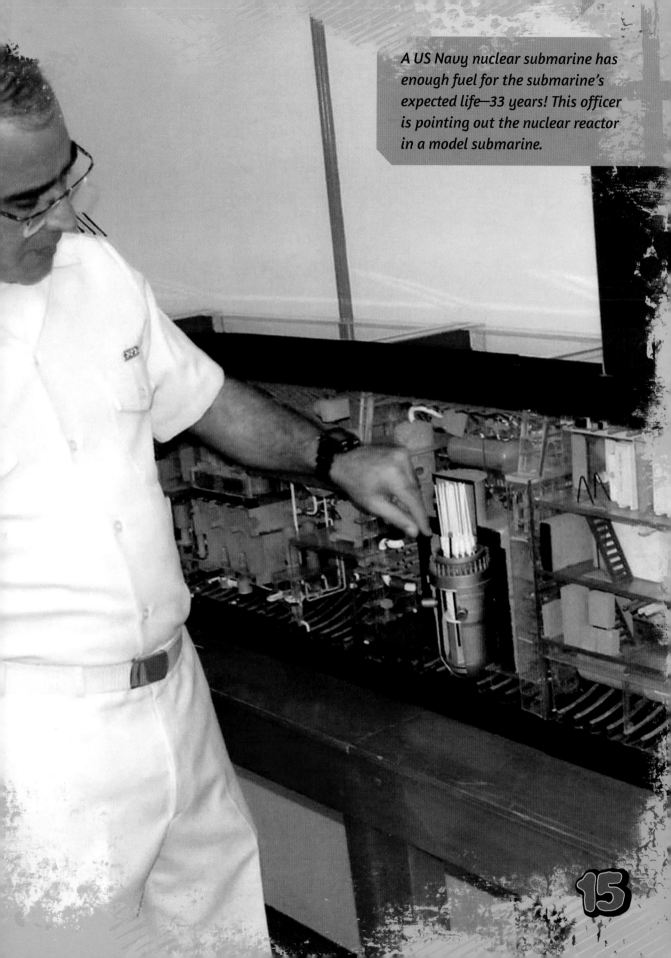

A US Navy nuclear submarine has enough fuel for the submarine's expected life—33 years! This officer is pointing out the nuclear reactor in a model submarine.

15

SSNs

SSN is the label for the US Navy's attack submarines. "SS" means "submarine," and "N" means "nuclear-powered." They're also called fast attacks or hunter-killers. As these names suggest, SSNs are meant to seek and destroy enemy submarines and surface ships. The submarines carry sensors to find enemy targets and guide weapons.

SSNs carry Tomahawk cruise missiles, which can be used to attack targets on shore and even objects hundreds of miles from the ocean! SSNs also lay mines underwater where enemy ships are likely to travel. When a ship makes contact, the mine explodes.

KINDS OF SSNS

The US Navy has three kinds of attack submarines in service today. The oldest and largest is the Los Angeles class. All these submarines are named after US cities. There are only three submarines in the Seawolf class. The newest group is the Virginia class. Most are named for US states.

missile-tube training tool ▶

The Virginia-class attack submarine Mississippi *during a test voyage in the Atlantic Ocean.*

SSBNs AND SSGNs

SSBNs are some of the most destructive vessels in the US Navy. SSBNs, nicknamed "boomers," each carry up to 24 nuclear missiles. A missile has several warheads that can be dropped on a number of targets. The SSBNs in service today belong to the Ohio class. They're each named for a US state except one—the USS *Henry M. Jackson*. Jackson was a US senator.

SSGN is the label for the navy's guided-missile submarines. These submarines are former SSBNs that have been changed, or altered, so they can carry conventional, or nonnuclear, missiles. The SSGNs have also been altered to transport up to 66 special operations soldiers along with the regular crew.

SEAL DELIVERY

Special operations forces include Navy SEAL (Sea, Air, and Land) teams who undertake extremely risky missions. SEALs often travel into dangerous territory to capture and kill enemies, collect information, and perform other duties. SSGNs can carry SEALs into territory in secrecy.

An unarmed missile launches from the USS Nevada.

19

THE COMMANDING OFFICER

Since submarines are some of the most dangerous military craft, they need a steady hand and a clear mind at the controls. The commanding officer is the leader who makes sure all systems on the submarine run smoothly. Before being appointed to this position, they spend time as the head of the engineering, weapons, and operations departments on both SSNs and SSBNs.

The commanding officer of a submarine is usually a commander or a lieutenant commander but is referred to as the captain. The commanding officer is sometimes one of the few people on the submarine who knows where the submarine is to be stationed during its time at sea.

THE XO

The second in command on a submarine is called the executive officer, or XO. While performing his regular duties, the XO also works on completing the requirements needed to be a submarine commanding officer. Only the commanding officer and executive officer of the submarine have private rooms, called staterooms, in which to work and sleep.

20

Most commanding officers are between 38 and 42 years old.

TO THE RESCUE

Even with a skilled crew and safety systems on board, things can still go wrong on submarines. In 1963, the US Navy submarine *Thresher* had an equipment failure near Cape Cod, Massachusetts. The reactor shut down, and the submarine sank to the bottom of the ocean. The water pressure destroyed the submarine. All 129 men aboard died.

In response, the navy built the DSRV, or Deep Submergence Rescue Vehicle. The DSRV can be brought anywhere in the world by airplane. Once at a location, it can rescue submarine crew as deep as 5,000 feet (1.5 km).

THE KURSK

In 2000, a Russian navy submarine called the *Kursk* sank, killing 118 men. It's thought that onboard torpedoes exploded. Poor sea conditions prevented any possible rescue. Some of the men left notes wrapped in plastic that were found later.

▲ ceremony honoring *Kursk* sailors

The DSRV has room for two pilots, two rescue crew, and 24 passengers.

DETECTED!

Because they're dangerous, submarines are one of the biggest enemy targets. There are several methods, besides sonar, to detect enemy submarines. Hydrophones, or underwater listening equipment, can be placed in the water. Aircraft may carry a Magnetic Anomaly Detector, or MAD, which locates a large amount of metal in water, such as the body of a submarine.

Once detected, a submarine faces several threats. Torpedoes may be fired from ships, submarines, or aircraft. The torpedo uses active sonar to find its underwater target. It doesn't even have to hit the submarine. An explosion near a submarine might be enough to destroy it.

THE ASROC

Another threat to a submarine is the ASROC, or Anti-Submarine Rocket. The ASROC is fired like a missile from a surface ship and enters the water near the target. Once in the water, it acts like a torpedo and races to the target.

A military helicopter may have a "dunking sonar" to dip into water to detect submarines.

25

OTHER UNDERWATER VESSELS

Military submarines aren't the only underwater vessels. Submarines are also used for studying the deepest parts of the ocean and the creatures that live there. Smaller submarines used for deep-sea exploration are called submersibles. Some submersibles travel to places even more extreme than military submarines.

In 1960, the *Trieste* took two men down to the Mariana Trench in the Pacific Ocean, the deepest part of any ocean in the world. They descended 35,800 feet (10,900 m). At the bottom, the two men in the *Trieste* saw a strange kind of fish. At that time, some scientists thought fish couldn't live at such depths.

the *Trieste*

THE TRIESTE

The *Trieste* wasn't a true submarine. It's called a bathyscaphe. It had a large chamber filled with gasoline, which is lighter than water, that helped it float. It also carried 9 tons (8.2 mt) of iron, which was heavy enough to bring the craft to the bottom. When the crew wanted to go back to the surface, they let go of the iron.

27

TAKE A TOUR

If you would like to know what it's like to serve on a submarine, there are places you can visit. The only submarine museum operated by the US Navy is the Submarine Force Museum. Located in Groton, Connecticut, the museum contains photographs and objects from the beginnings of the US Navy's submarine force to the present day.

At the museum, you can also tour the *Nautilus*, the first nuclear submarine and the first to visit the North Pole. And if you can't go to the museum, you can take an online tour on their website—www.ussnautilus.org!

USS *Nautilus*

THE NAUTILUS

The *Nautilus* joined the US Navy in 1954. In 1958, it was the first submarine to reach the North Pole, which was thought to be impossible at the time. Over the course of its 25 years of active service, the *Nautilus* traveled more than 500,000 miles (804,500 km)!

The Los Angeles-class attack submarine USS Annapolis passes by the USS Nautilus as it makes its way up the Thames River in Connecticut.

INDEX